ANIMAL SURVIVAL

HIDING AND BLUFFING TO SURVIVE

BY PARKER HOLMES

CONTENT CONSULTANT
EVAN KRISTIANSEN, PhD
LECTURER IN BIOLOGY
BOSTON UNIVERSITY

Kids Core

An Imprint of Abdo Publishing
abdobooks.com

abdobooks.com

Published by Abdo Publishing, a division of ABDO, PO Box 398166, Minneapolis, Minnesota 55439. Copyright © 2023 by Abdo Consulting Group, Inc. International copyrights reserved in all countries. No part of this book may be reproduced in any form without written permission from the publisher. Kids Core™ is a trademark and logo of Abdo Publishing.

Printed in the United States of America, North Mankato, Minnesota.
052022
092022

THIS BOOK CONTAINS
RECYCLED MATERIALS

Cover Photo: Shutterstock Images
Interior Photos: Shutterstock Images, 4–5, 22, 25 (top), 25 (bottom), 29 (top); Jonathan Hernould/Shutterstock Images, 7; Jamikorn Sooktaramorn/Shutterstock Images, 8; Christopher Moswitzer/iStockphoto, 10–11; Andrei Stepanov/Shutterstock Images, 13, 28 (top); Cheryl Ramalho/iStockphoto, 14; iStockphoto, 15; Jiri Balek/Shutterstock Images, 16, 28 (bottom); Kurit Afshen/Shutterstock Images, 17; Mark Brandon/Shutterstock Images, 18; Vittorio Bruno/Shutterstock Images, 20–21; Moize Nicolas/Shutterstock Images, 24; Gorilla Images/Shutterstock Images, 26, 29 (bottom)

Editor: Ann Schwab
Series Designer: Katharine Hale

Library of Congress Control Number: 2021951652

Publisher's Cataloging-in-Publication Data

Names: Holmes, Parker, author.
Title: Hiding and bluffing to survive / by Parker Holmes
Description: Minneapolis, Minnesota : Abdo Publishing, 2023 | Series: Animal survival | Includes online resources and index.
Identifiers: ISBN 9781532198519 (lib. bdg.) | ISBN 9781644947685 (pbk.) | ISBN 9781098272166 (ebook)
Subjects: LCSH: Animal defenses--Juvenile literature. | Defense measures--Juvenile literature. | Adaptation (Physiology)--Juvenile literature. | Animal behavior--Juvenile literature.
Classification: DDC 591.57--dc23

CONTENTS

Some animals need to hide to avoid being eaten by other animals, such as sharks.

CHAPTER 1

UNDERWATER ESCAPE

A shark is on the hunt. An octopus senses danger. But there is no time to swim away. The octopus uses a **camouflage** trick to change color. It is now the same color as the surrounding coral. The shark swims past the octopus and never sees it.

The shark seems to have been fooled. The octopus starts moving again. But the hungry shark circles back and sees the octopus. It is too late to hide. So the octopus uses another survival **tactic**. It spreads its arms to look bigger. It also turns a lighter color. The shark is surprised. This gives the octopus just enough time to swim away. It hides safely in the coral.

Cephalopod Camouflage

Cephalopods are experts at hiding. These animals include octopuses, squids, and cuttlefish. They can change color in less than one second. Some even change their skin textures. A cuttlefish, for example, can make itself look like a bumpy rock!

Octopuses can spread their arms and turn colors to escape predators.

Survival Tricks

The octopus escaped the shark by using the survival strategies of hiding and bluffing. Lots of animals hide. They do it to escape hungry **predators**.

The orchid mantis uses camouflage to disguise itself as a flower while it watches for prey.

Animals also hide to find food. Hiding makes it easier to catch prey. Animals often use camouflage to stay hidden as they hunt. They use color and shape to disguise themselves.

Some animals also do the opposite of hiding. They bluff by pretending to be something they're not. These animals make themselves look bigger or scarier than they are to frighten predators. This is called a **startle display**. Bluffing is another way animals survive.

Octopuses are masters of disguise. Jon Ablett, curator at the National History Museum in the United Kingdom, explains octopus camouflage:

> Thousands of specialized cells under their skin, called chromatophores, help them to change color in an instant.

Source: Lisa Hendry. "Octopuses Keep Surprising Us." *National History Museum*, n.d., nhm.ac.uk. Accessed 29 Dec. 2021.

What's the Big Idea?

Read this quote carefully. What is its main idea? Explain how the main idea is supported by details.

A snake hides in a tree branch, watching for prey.

CHAPTER 2

HIDING OUT

Not all animals can protect themselves with sharp teeth or fast legs. Many animals avoid danger by hiding. Hiding also helps animals catch prey.

Animals hide in different ways. Some use actual hiding places.

Animals such as monkeys and rodents hide in the treetops of rain forests. Other animals hide by staying very still. Rabbits will freeze in place to reduce the chance of being spotted by a hawk.

Animals also use camouflage to avoid being seen. Their colors and shapes help them blend in with their surroundings. Animals such as arctic hares use camouflage. Arctic hares are brown in warm months. This makes them hard to see against the ground. But in winter their fur turns white. This makes hares look like snow. Predators have a harder time finding the hares when they match their environment.

The arctic hare's winter fur allows it to blend into its snowy surroundings.

The leopard's spots make it possible to hide in plain sight.

Big cats such as leopards and jaguars also have colored coats for camouflage. They have dark spots on their fur. The spots break up the shape of the cats. The spots also help the animals blend in with the forest as light filters

The flounder uses both its shape and color to hide as it waits for prey.

through the trees. The camouflaged coats help the cats sneak up on prey.

Camouflage Superpowers

Some animals, such as the flounder, use both color and shape to survive. A flounder is a flat fish that lives at the bottom of the sea. It changes colors to match the seafloor. The flounder's disguise keeps it safe. The camouflage also helps it hunt. When a fish swims by, the hidden flounder will **ambush** it.

The leaf-tailed gecko is a master at camouflage.

The leaf-tailed gecko is one of the world's best hiders. These geckos use both color and shape. Their skin can look like bark or dead leaves. They also can flatten their bodies.

Male panther chameleons display vibrant colors to find mates.

When they are resting on trees or leaves, they are hard to spot. They almost disappear.

Colorful Chameleons

Chameleons are famous for changing colors. These lizards can turn green, brown, and other colors. But chameleons mostly do not change colors for camouflage. They usually do it to communicate with other chameleons. Some turn brighter colors to attract a mate.

Stick insects can appear to be part of a tree. This helps them hide from predators.

Lots of predators eat insects. That is why so many insects use camouflage. Stick insects are great at hiding. These insects are also called walking sticks. They are long and skinny and usually brown or green. They actually look like sticks! Their shape and color protect them from being spotted. A predator might think the stick insect is just a twig.

Further Evidence

Look at the website below. Does it give any new evidence to support Chapter Two?

Wacky Weekend: Hidden Animals

abdocorelibrary.com/hiding-and-bluffing-to-survive

Octopuses can shoot ink to startle predators. This gives them time to escape.

CHAPTER 3

A BIG SURPRISE

Some animals use a survival trick that is the opposite of hiding. They make themselves look bigger and scarier. This bluffing can frighten and confuse predators. Startle displays can give animals time to escape.

The cobra can frighten away predators by creating a hood.

Cobras are famous for making themselves look bigger. When **threatened**, a cobra lifts its head and neck into the air. Then it spreads its neck. It does this by stretching the skin around its neck. This forms a hood. The hood makes the cobra look bigger. This helps it scare away predators.

Some fish know how to turn away attackers too. Puffer fish are not always fast enough to swim from danger. So, they make themselves much bigger. They do this by sucking in water and sometimes air. This blows them up to more than twice their normal size.

Insect or Leaf?

Some animals are good at both bluffing and hiding. Katydids have both skills. These insects are often the same color and shape as leaves. If a predator does find them, katydids will startle the attacker. Some katydids can open their wings to flash bright colors and markings that look like eyes.

Puffer fish can blow themselves up to more than double their normal size. This bluffing tactic makes them less attractive to predators.

Predators think swollen puffer fish do not look easy to eat, so they leave them alone.

Frilled lizards also know how to make themselves look scarier. If threatened, they open their mouths. Then they raise the skin around their necks. Their neck frills quickly pop up. This makes their heads look much larger. Then they hiss and stand upright. This could be a scary sight to a predator!

Frilled Lizard Bluffing

Frill down

Frill raised

These photos show how frilled lizards use bluffing. When the lizards feel threatened, they raise their frills. This makes them look larger. This can scare away predators.

The large eyespots on this peacock butterfly can help protect it against predators.

Shocking Behavior

Animals sometimes flash bright colors or patterns to frighten away predators. Many moths and butterflies have patterns on their wings that resemble eyes. These are called eyespots. Predators may see these eyespots and think the prey animal is much larger than it is. Some moths and butterflies have their eyespots hidden on their hind wings and will flash predators to startle them away.

Some **species** of praying mantises also flash colors. The insects stand tall and stretch out their arms and wings to look bigger. Then the mantises show off bright colors on their undersides.

Animals live in a dangerous world. They need many skills to stay alive. Hiding and bluffing are two skills animals use to survive.

Explore Online

Visit the website below. Does it give any new information about how cobras protect themselves that wasn't in Chapter Three?

King Cobra

abdocorelibrary.com/hiding-and -bluffing-to-survive

SURVIVAL FACTS

Many animals use color for camouflage.

Some animals use both color and shape for camouflage.

Animals sometimes bluff by making themselves look bigger.

Some animals bluff by flashing bright colors and patterns.

Glossary

ambush
a surprise attack made from a hidden place

camouflage
coloring or another feature that allows animals to blend
into their surroundings

predator
an animal that hunts other animals for food

species
groups of similar living things that can have
young together

startle display
bluffing behavior by an animal that changes its features to
scare away predators

tactic
a way of doing something; a method

threatened
feeling as if one is in danger

Online Resources

To learn more about hiding and bluffing to survive, visit our free resource websites below.

Visit **abdocorelibrary.com** or scan this QR code for free Common Core resources for teachers and students, including vetted activities, multimedia, and booklinks, for deeper subject comprehension.

Visit **abdobooklinks.com** or scan this QR code for free additional online weblinks for further learning. These links are routinely monitored and updated to provide the most current information available.

Learn More

Murray, Julie. *Jaguars*. Abdo, 2020.

Reeves, Josette. *How Not to Get Eaten*. DK, 2022.

Thomas, Rachael L. *Animal Camouflage Clash*. Abdo, 2020.

Index

About the Author

Parker Holmes has written numerous nonfiction books for children on subjects ranging from snakes to sports. He especially likes writing books about animals. He and his family live in Daphne, Alabama.